SENATE

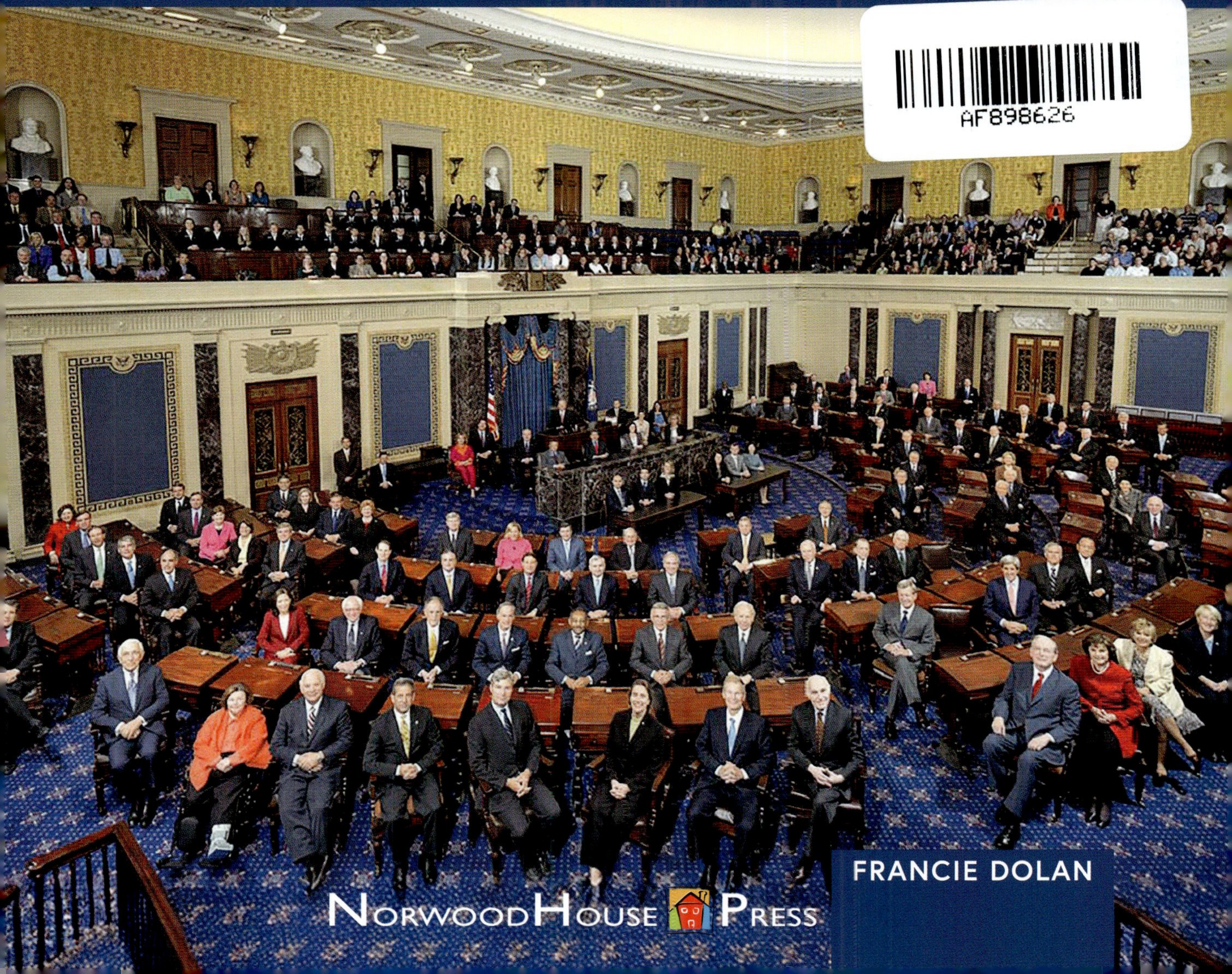

FRANCIE DOLAN

NorwoodHouse Press

Cataloging-in-Publication Data

Names: Dolan, Francie.
Title: Senate / Francie Dolan.
Description: Buffalo, NY : Norwood House Press, 2027. | Series: The United States government | Includes glossary and index.
Identifiers: ISBN 9781978581555 (pbk.) | ISBN 9781978581562 (library bound) | ISBN 9781978581579 (ebook)
Subjects: LCSH: United States. Congress. Senate--Juvenile literature. | Legislators--United States--Juvenile literature. | Legislation--United States--Juvenile literature.
Classification: LCC JK1276.D65 2027 | DDC 328.73071--dc23

Published in 2027 by
Norwood House Press
2544 Clinton Street
Buffalo, NY 14224

Designer: Rhea Magaro
Editor: Tricia Hoffman

Photo credits: Cover, p. 1 VectorMine/Shutterstock.com; cover, p. 1 Sergey Kamshylin/Shutterstock.com; p. 5 VectorMine/Shutterstock.com; pp. 6, 21 Wikipedia; pp. 7, 8 Library of Congress; p. 9 DenysHolovatiuk/Shutterstock.com; p. 10 Volodymyr TVERDOKHLIB/Shutterstock.com; p. 12 Wikipedia; p. 13 John Ramspott; p. 14 Zachary Hupp/Shutterstock.com; p. 15 Benjamin Applebaum/Shutterstock.com; p. 16 Ron Adar/Shutterstock.com; p. 17 The White House; p. 18 Javanism/Shutterstock.com; p. 19 Sundry Photography/Shutterstock.com;

Printed in the United States of America

CPSIA compliance information: Batch #CSNHP27: For further information contact Norwood House Press at 1-800-237-9932.

TABLE OF CONTENTS

THE UNITED STATES GOVERNMENT

The United States **Constitution** tells how the nation's government is organized. There are three parts, or branches. They are the executive branch, **legislative** branch, and judicial branch.

The Senate is part of the legislative branch.

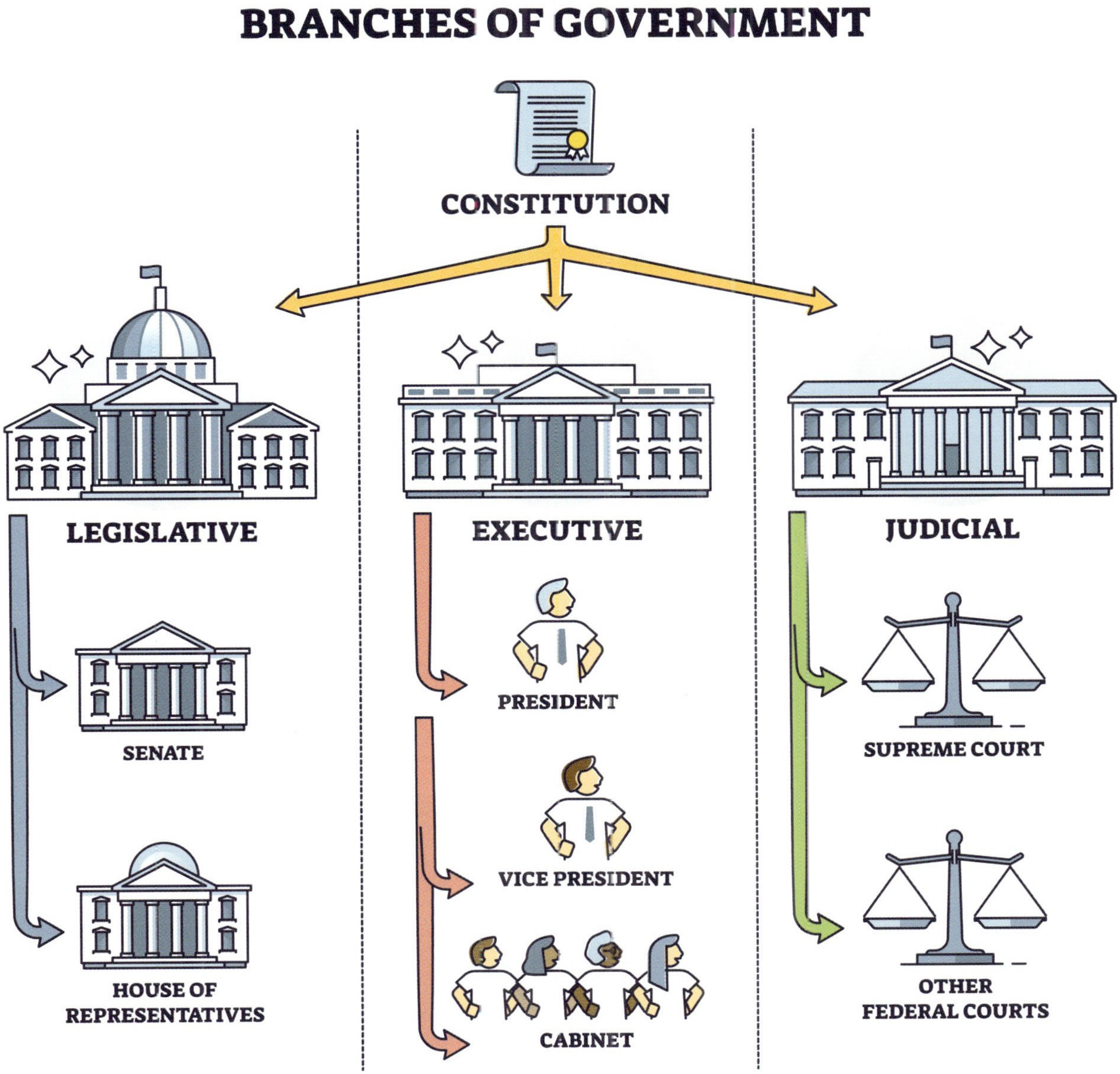
BRANCHES OF GOVERNMENT
CONSTITUTION
LEGISLATIVE
EXECUTIVE
JUDICIAL
SENATE
HOUSE OF REPRESENTATIVES
PRESIDENT
VICE PRESIDENT
CABINET
SUPREME COURT
OTHER FEDERAL COURTS

THE UPPER HOUSE

The writers of the U.S. Constitution had to decide how people would be represented by legislators in **Congress** to vote on laws for the country.

States with many people wanted representation to be based on population. Small states did not want to be ignored.

The Great **Compromise** settled the issue. Congress would have two parts, or houses. Legislators in the House of Representatives, or Lower House, would be based on population.

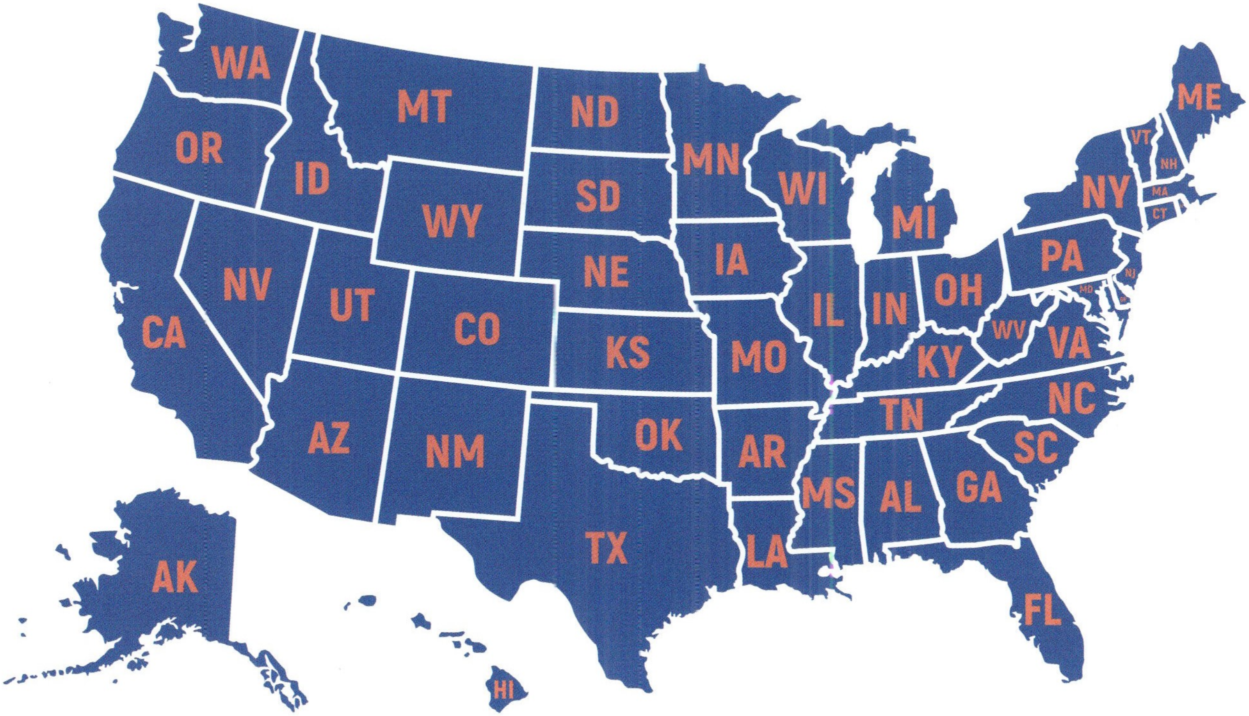

Legislators in the Senate, or Upper House, would be based on states. Each state, no matter how big or small, would get two senators. Congress still works this way today.

The Senate meets in one wing of the U.S. Capitol Building in Washington, D.C. When an American flag flies over that side of the building, the Senate is in session.

There are 50 states, so the Senate has 100 members. If a vote is split 50-50, the U.S. vice president votes to break the tie.

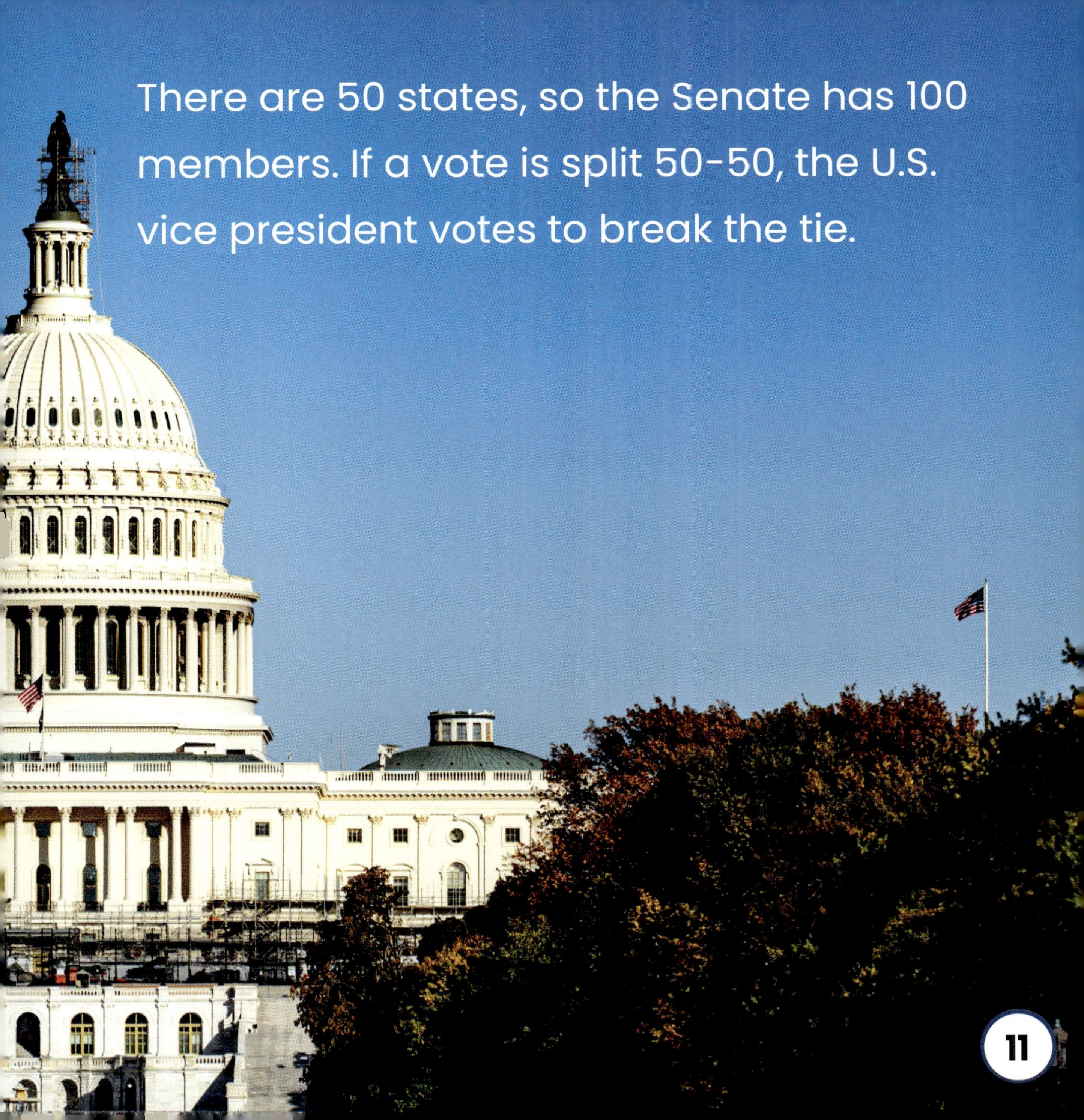

Senators are elected for six-year **terms**. There is no limit on how many terms they can serve.

Senators must be at least 30 years old. They must be U.S. citizens. They must live in the state they represent.

POWERS AND RESPONSIBILITIES

Senators work in **committees** to understand the needs of the country. They write **bills** to suggest new laws. Each senator has a staff to help.

Senate leaders, including the Majority Leader, decide which bills go to the Senate floor for **debate** and voting.

If a bill passes the Senate, it goes to the House of Representatives for a vote. Before a bill can become law, both houses must pass it.

The U.S. president signs the approved bill. Then, it is a new law. If the president will not sign, and two-thirds of Congress still votes yes, the bill becomes law.

The Senate has special duties. It checks many decisions made by the president. It approves or rejects the president's choices for officials, judges, and treaties with other countries.

Along with the Lower House, the Senate has the power to declare war. It can **impeach** the president.

GOVERNING THE UNITED STATES

Senators have important jobs. They represent their **constituents**. They make laws. They check the president's power.

Which two senators are from your state? How do their decisions affect you?

GLOSSARY

bills (bilz): written plans for new laws to be debated and voted on by legislators

committees (kuh-MIT-eez): groups of people chosen to discuss issues and make decisions for a larger group; Senate committees include the Foreign Relations Committee and the Veterans' Affairs Committee

compromise (KAHM-pruh-mize): an agreement that accepts something that is not entirely what you wanted in order to satisfy some of the requests of other people

Congress (KAHNG-gris): the part of the U.S. government that makes laws and that includes the House of Representatives and the Senate; the legislative body of the United States

constituents (kuhn-STICH-oo-uhnts): voters represented by an elected official; people who live in the state represented by a senator

constitution (kahn-sti-TOO-shuhn): a document that sets forth the basic laws of a country and that outlines the rights of its people and the power of its government

debate (di-BATE): discussion in which people express different opinions and ideas

impeach (im-PEECH): to remove an official from their position for breaking a rule or committing a crime

legislative (lej-is-LAY-tive): related to the branch of government that makes and changes laws for the country

terms (turmz): definite or set periods of time; U.S. senators are elected to terms that last six years

THINKING QUESTIONS

1. Which branch of the U.S. government includes the Senate?

2. What was the Great Compromise?

3. How many senators are in the Senate? Why?

4. How does a bill become a law?

5. How does the Senate check the powers of the president?

INDEX

ABOUT THE AUTHOR

Francie Dolan is a writer from Seattle, Washington. She is an American history buff who loves to learn about how her country works and how it has changed over time. She jumps at the chance to travel to Washington, D.C., and visit the capital's important buildings and monuments.